Healthy Kids

Keeping Fit

Sylvia Goulding

CHERRYTREE
BOOKS

Published in 2006 by The Evans Publishing Group
2A Portman Mansions
Chiltern Steet
London W1U 6NR

Reprinted in 2007

Printed in China

British Library Cataloguing in Publication Data

Goulding, Sylvia
  Keeping fit. - (Healthy kids)
  1.Health - Juvenile literature 2.Exercise - Juvenile
  literature
  I.Title
  613.7

ISBN-10 paperback:	1842343157
ISBN-13 paperback:	9781842343159
ISBN-10 hardback:	1842344099
ISBN-13 hardback:	9781842344095

PHOTOGRAPHIC CREDITS
Cover: **RubberBall**
Title page: **RubberBall**
BananaStock: 5, 13, 21, 22, 26; **The Brown Reference Group plc**: 17, Edward Allwright 9, 20, 26; **Corbis**: 11, 16; **Hemera Photo Objects**: 4, 6, 8, 14, 15, 17, 18, 21, 22, 23, 25, 27; **RubberBall**: 3, 5, 6, 7, 10, 11, 12, 13, 17, 23, 28, 29; Paralyzed Veterans of America, by permission of **Sports 'N Spokes**: 24.

FOR THE EVANS PUBLISHING GROUP

Editor: **Louise John**
Production: **Jenny Mulvanny**
Design: **D. R. ink**
Consultant: **Dr. Julia Dalton BM DCH**

FOR THE BROWN REFERENCE GROUP PLC

Art Editor: **Norma Martin**
Managing Editor: **Bridget Giles**

With thanks to models **Isabella Farnhell, Lydia O'Neill and Sam Thomson**

Important note: Healthy Kids encourages readers to actively pursue good health for life. All information in Healthy Kids is for educational purposes only. For specific and personal medical advice, diagnoses, treatment and exercise and diet advice, consult your doctor.

Some words are shown in bold, **like this**. You can find out what they mean by looking in the glossary on page 30.

Contents

◄You don't have to be a professional athlete. Simple and fun ball games can put you on the road to fitness.

Get fit for life
...and have lots of fun

fit children are usually also healthy children. If you're fit, you can do everyday things easily. You can run, climb stairs or ride a bicycle. Regular physical **activity** makes your muscles and bones strong. It gives you bundles of energy and a healthy **heart** and **lungs**. It's amazing, but getting active can even make you happy. The activity sends a lot of feel-good messages around your body. Best of all, getting fit is fun!

Just amazing!

Physical activity can even make you think better. Blood carries **oxygen** to your brain. Your brain needs oxygen for thinking. When you exercise, your heart works harder. It pumps blood around your body faster. This gets more oxygen to your brain.

Unfit is dangerous

Children who are unfit have a difficult time staying healthy. Sitting around and doing nothing all day leaves some parts of the body under-used. Unfit children can become overweight. They might get all sorts of health problems and serious illnesses. They can suffer from **diabetes** or **asthma**. They can get heart problems or crumbly bones later in life. They can also miss out on many exciting and fun activities.

◄► Getting active is a great way to make new friends, whatever you do.

You can skip, splash in a swimming pool, have a fun bicycle race or try a trampoline.

Skipping is active and great fun. You can try fancy double Dutch jumps with your friends.

How fit are you?

t ry the simple activities in the box on page 7 and find out how fit you are. Write down on a piece of paper each activity you try. Give yourself a star for each one that you can do. Not many stars? Time to get active and fit!

◄ *Being active includes things other than sports. A majorette exercises her muscles and heart as she twirls a baton and marches with a band.*

Or try this...

Keep a fitness diary
● Write down for one week how much time you are being active (doing sports, walking, running).

● Write down for each day how much time you are not active (watching TV, playing video games or on a computer, eating, reading).

Test yourself

Keeping going
- **Arms:** Swim a width in a pool as fast as you can. (Make sure an adult is with you).
- **Legs:** Climb three flights of stairs without stopping.
- **Body:** Dance to music for ten minutes.
Out of breath? Improve your fitness.

Being flexible
- **Arms:** Touch your hands behind your back, one arm going up over your shoulder.
- **Legs:** Sit down. Pull first one, then the other foot right up to touch your chin.
- **Body:** Stand up straight. Bend sideways to the left until your left hand reaches your left knee.

Now bend to the right and touch your right knee.
Couldn't do it? Get more flexible.

Being strong
- **Arms:** Pick up two heavy books. Hold them out in front of you, with both arms outstretched. Now slowly count to ten.
- **Legs:** Stand against a wall. Slide down a short way so your knees are bent. Slowly count to ten.
- **Body:** Lie down, with knees bent. Stay in this position. Now do a half sit-up. Slowly count to ten.
Couldn't do it? Build some muscle and get more fit all over.

▼ *Sit opposite a friend, feet touching. Now pull each other forwards.*

- Add up how many hours you were active or not active. If your activity total is less than seven hours, you need to get active.

Back to basics
Are you sitting comfortably?

a long row of bones runs down the centre of your back. It's called your **spine**. Your spine holds your body in position. It carries your head, which weighs as much as five or six large tin cans! Most people spend a lot of time sitting down. Many people slouch. Look in a mirror and check the way you sit. Are you leaning forwards? Or are you slumped back?

▲ If you always slouch on your seat, you get backache. Your back will become rounded, too.

Safety first!

Don't get lop-sided...
- Carry a heavy school bag on your back and not in one hand.
- To pick up a heavy object, bend your knees. Keep your back straight.

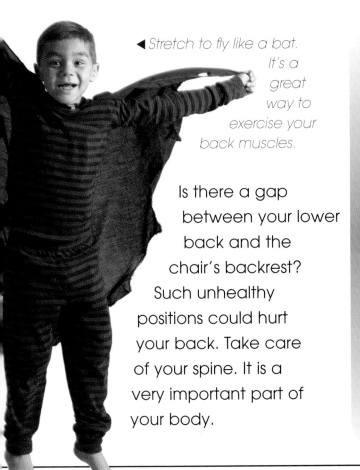

◀ Stretch to fly like a bat. It's a great way to exercise your back muscles.

Is there a gap between your lower back and the chair's backrest? Such unhealthy positions could hurt your back. Take care of your spine. It is a very important part of your body.

Sitting pretty

To sit well, slide your buttocks as far back in the chair as is comfortable. Lean back so your back is supported by the chair. Tuck a small cushion into the small of your back for extra support. Hold your back and neck straight. Keep your head above the spine. If your desk is too high or too low to place your arms on top, make your seat higher or lower.

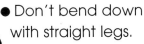

- Don't bend down with straight legs.
- Walk with a straight back, too. It makes you tall and healthy.

Why is it good for me?
- If you don't stand, walk, bend and sit straight, your back muscles will get weak, your bones will be hunched and the inside of your stomach will feel cramped.

Get active

...get up and get moving now

are your face and fingers the only active parts of your body? Stop being a couch potato now. There are lots of ways to get active. Even if you don't like school sports, there's something you'll like doing. Just try out different things. Be active every day, and be active for at least 20 minutes.

◄ *Playing with a ball makes you move and keeps you fit. It's great fun, too!*

Getting ready ...

Or try this...

When you're by yourself...
- Play with a ball in the garden.
- Invent some new dance steps.
- Hop on one leg.

When you're with a friend...
- Play table tennis.
- Practise handstands.
- Wash a neighbour's car, but ask first!

Stretch and go

A mega-stretch session will get you going

1- Hair this long...
Stretch your arms as wide as you can, feet apart. Bend at the waist, to the right and to the left.

2- Star jump
Jump in the air with your arms and feet as far apart as you can.

3- Take this!
Kick one leg high in the air, arms apart. Now kick the other one.

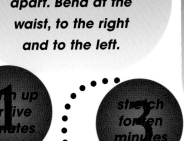

warm up for five minutes

stretch for ten minutes

walk, jog, or bicycle so you feel warm

Are you too tired for sports? It's strange but true that if you force yourself to get active, you'll suddenly feel full of energy!

When there's a crowd of you...
- Play tag or hide-and-seek.
- Have a game of football.
- Compete in a three-legged race.

Always active
...come rain or shine

there's no excuse – you can be active anytime and any place. If it rains, you can tumble on the floor. Have a pillow fight in the bedroom or balance along the edge of a rug. Kick a balloon around. Practise dance steps or karate moves.

◀ *Practise with a hula hoop. See who can keep it up longest!*

▶ *'I'll get it!' Jump on your scooter and run an errand.*

Quiz -?-?-?-?-?

1 The best way to get fit is:
A ...to watch sports on TV or to go and watch a football match.
B ...to exercise every day, for at least 20 or 30 minutes at a time.

2 If you exercise often:
A Your heart and lungs work hard and get strong.
B You will suffer from heart disease as an adult.

Skipping is for champions. Even boxers skip

r super-fitness. Why not set up a skipping competition?

Or try this...

In the heat of the day...
- *practise different swim strokes*
- *play with water balloons*

Make sure you're with an adult!

In ice and snow...
- *pull a friend on a toboggan*
- *build giant snowmen*

Dress warmly when it's cold!

3 True or false?
You need at least five people to play sports or do exercises.
A True
B False

ANSWERS: 1B, 2A, 3B.

Get strong

Strong muscles give you power. They let you do energetic things, such as climbing, cycling, dancing and rowing, for longer. They also help protect your bones and **joints**. Joints are the 'hinges' where your bones join. It's easy to train muscles. You can make them stronger without being a bodybuilder.

◄ Ask your parents if you can cycle to see a friend. It will give you strong legs. Make sure you wear a helmet for extra protection!

nearly half your body is muscle

Or try this...

When there's two or a few of you...

● Do the wheelbarrrow walk: walk on your hands, while a friend holds your legs!
● Who can hop longest on one leg? Try it when the TV adverts are on.

Muscling in

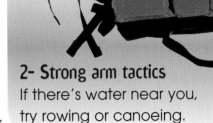

 you have 600 muscles

1- Power up your legs

Get out of the car and rollerblade or skateboard in the park. Or run up the stairs instead of using the lift.

2- Strong arm tactics

If there's water near you, try rowing or canoeing.

3- Awesome stomach muscles

Sit on a chair. Pull your legs up with knees bent and stay like that for as long as you can. Or lie on your stomach. Raise your arms and legs off the floor. Keep them up for as long as you can.

Safety

Make sure a responsible adult is with you at all times.

Always wear proper sports equipment. Helmets, elbow pads and knee pads protect you if you fall.

Take care near traffic.

strongest muscle the tongue!

When there's a crowd of you...

● Play tug-of-war: Set up two teams. Make them roughly matched for size and strength. Draw a line on the ground. Line up the teams either side of the line. Mark the centre of a rope with a coloured band. On 'Go!' each team pulls on the rope as hard as they can. They try to pull the other team across the line. This fun game strengthens arms, legs and body.

Keep your balance
...and don't fall over

even if you don't want to become a tightrope walker, a good sense of balance is important. It stops you falling when you run over uneven ground. It lets you reach for a very low tennis ball. It helps you walk over a slippery surface. Your body balances itself all the time. Normally you only notice this when things go wrong. Then you might fall or feel dizzy.

Dizzy feelings

◀ *Try skateboarding for balance. But always wear a helmet, knee and elbow pads to protect yourself.*

Or try this

Wobbly games...
● Play flamingoes: Stand on one leg. Cross the other leg over in front you. Stand like this for five minutes, without putting the second leg down.

● Stand on one leg again. Close your eyes. Do you feel all wobbly?
● Stand on a soft surface such as a foam mat. Now try again. Still standing?
● Stand on one leg and catch a ball.

Just amazing!

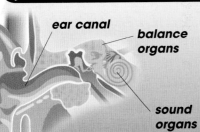

ear canal

balance organs

sound organs

Do you know where your sense of balance is? There are important balance **organs** in your inner ears! That is why an ear infection can make you feel dizzy.

Walk the line

Draw a chalk line on the pavement and balance along that. Do you feel all wobbly and drift off the line? To help you balance, stretch your arms away from your body like aeroplane wings.

...after spinning around

...wearing blindfolds

...with an ear infection

When there's a crowd of you...

● Blindfold one person at a time. Tell them how to walk around chairs in the room. In the summer, make them walk around trees in the park.

● You need a sense of balance for many sports on water, on ice or with moving parts. Try surfing, ice skating or skateboarding.

Stay flexible

You're probably fairly flexible. Most children are. You need to keep your body active so it doesn't get stiff and 'rusty' like an old car as you grow up. Martial arts can help you fight off stiffness. Most make your body flexible. They also give you strength and make you feel confident. There are many different styles. For example, try kung fu or kickboxing. Go for karate or tae kwon do. Or you can learn kendo, jujitsu, judo or tai chi. There are many more, and one will be right for you.

◀▶ *Tae kwon do is fast and exciting. You get fit, strong and flexible*

Just amazing!

People who are more flexible than others are often called double-jointed. Some appear in circus acts as contortionists. These people can bend and stretch into all sorts of strange positions.

Daniel Browning Smith is known as the rubber boy. He was in the *Guinness Book of Records* twice and holds the World Record for cramming himself into a tiny box, measuring just 46 x 41 centimetres!

Stretch and bend and dance...

One of the most fun ways to bend your body is with music. Just get into the groove and follow the rhythm. Swing your arms, turn your head and move your legs about. Bend at your waist, jump up and twist around. Pretend you're a famous pop star or a dancer. It won't even feel like exercise.

Whether you like hip hop or pop, salsa or ballet – listen to the music and move.

Or try this...

Easy ways to become more flexible...
- Tumble around the floor as if you were being blown around by a hurricane.
- If it snows, reach for the snowflakes. If it rains, reach for raindrops.

- Limbo dance under a clothes line. How close can you get to the ground?
- Play basketball or netball.
- Yoga is a gentle way to get flexible. Learn it in a class from a good teacher.

Quick
...as a flash

races are a great way to develop speed and give you bundles of energy. You don't need to be an Olympic champion. There are all sorts of races. There are running races, over short and long distances. You can run over hurdles, cross country or in a relay. Or you could race each other in the swimming pool, in the park or on rollerblades or skateboards.

Running facts

▲ *Run as fast as you can. It's a great way to work your heart and lungs.*

Or try this...

When you're on your own...
● When it's hot, race yourself in the swimming pool. Lie on your back and use your hands to paddle toward your feet. Next time do it faster.

● Bottom shuffle: Slide backward on your bottom. Use your hands to move along.
● Invent a funny walk. Raise one knee and clap your hands under it, then raise the other knee.

The fastest creature on the ground is the tiger beetle. In one second, it can run 125 times as far as it is long. For you that would be 150 metres!

Personal best

You can even compete against yourself. How? Just measure the time it takes you to do something. Each time you do it, try to better that time. How long does it take you to reach the end of the swimming pool wearing flippers?

◀ Use a stopwatch to time a race.

When there's two or more of you...

● Back-to-back race: Compete as pairs. Each pair is tied back to back.
● In a shallow pool, race each other on floats or inflatable lilos.

● In the snow, try to build the tallest and fattest snowman in ten minutes.
● Run a three-legged race. Two children tie the right leg of one to the left leg of the other. Then run as a pair.

Winner takes all?

Competing against each other is fun. The whole sports world is full of competitions. Just think of the Olympic Games or the World Cup. You can train your body to become stronger and faster. You can also train your mind to help you win competitions. Before a competition, try out the race course or playing field if you can. Now prepare your

◄ *Winning first prize or a medal is great. It makes you feel proud. But don't be nasty to other children who don't win!*

1 If you win first prize, you should...
A laugh at the losers
B be happy and friendly
C throw the medal away

2 If you lose a competition, you should...
A practise to get better
B go away and cry
C shout at the winner

ANSWERS: 1B, 2A.

Remember, you are playing to have fun, not just to win.

mind. Relax, breathe deeply and imagine that you are taking part in the competition. Imagine the whole game, and every move. Imagine making a mistake. Then correct the mistake in your mind until all runs smoothly. Practise winning in your mind.

Before the game, eat well and sleep well. Then say to yourself: 'I can do this, and I will do it'. Repeat this in your mind. Go out there and try your best. Good luck!

Losing out

...and too much pressure
What if you never, ever win? Don't worry, because losing can be good for you. You can find out where your weaknesses are. You can practise and train to become better. If you're playing team sports, ask your friends to help you. Don't blame others. Try to find out why you are not winning. Perhaps you'd rather try a different sport?

Or try this...

You cannot lose if you...
- Go for a jog. Keep going for as long as possible.
- Go trampolining.
- Weed the garden.
- Go for a long walk in the countryside.
- Climb a tree.
- Help your mum or dad do the chores.

Disability
...does not have to hold you back

if you cannot run or jump or you have poor eyesight or hearing, there are still many sports you can do. A sports wheelchair will let you play team games such as basketball. A special lift can lower you into a swimming pool or lift you onto a horse. There are special skis and bikes, too. Often it helps to change the rules a little and it's always a good idea to have an experienced and responsible adult there to help and guide you.

◄ *A sports wheelchair can help you become a champion of the racetrack.*

What to do...

With a friend in a wheelchair...
● go fishing
● arm-wrestle
● Cheer on your team.

With a hearing-impaired friend...
● Water the plants in the garden.
● Play basketball or beachball.
● Go for a long hike in the country.
● Throw snowballs for target practice.

Helping others
...get the best out of life

Sight-impaired children can run and swim. Some can even cycle or ski, if they have a guide. Many have some eyesight and can see bright balls, ropes, mats or field markers.

Make games easier for everyone to play. Fit the goal with a buzzer so you can hear where it is.

Use a ball with bells and wear wristbands with bells, so you can hear where the other players and the ball are.

Guides help in the swimming pool. They can gently tap a child with poor sight on the head when he or she reaches the end of a swimming lane.

Gymnastics and dance are also great for partially sighted children.

Children with hearing problems can join in most games and sports. But don't just call signals or commands – give a clear sign that people can see. Use a flag or a signal light, for example.

Safety first!
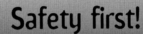

Before starting any games or activities, make sure that you are all familiar with the room and that no toys or furniture are lying around.

With a sight-impaired friend...

● Play goalball: There are two teams of three players. Players are sight-impaired or blindfolded. The ball has a bell in it so you can hear it. Each team tries to throw the ball at the wall behind the other team. The other team tries to stop them.
● Wash and groom the dog.
● Ride a tandem bike.
● Dance together to music.

▲ *Sport and games are exhausting. Give your body a chance to recover and get its strength back.*

After exercise ...make sure you chill out

Cooling down after energetic activities is just as important as warming up before. Finish your exercise session with five minutes of slow and easy movements. Walk slowly. Or stand on one spot and lift first one knee, then the other. Do some arm, leg and body stretches. It makes your heart rate slow down and return to normal. It also relaxes your muscles. And it stops your muscles feeling sore the day after.

Quiz -?-?-?-?-?

1 After a game of football, you should...
A Run home and watch TV.
B Go to a burger bar. Eat as much as you can load on your plate.
C Drink plenty of water.

2 The best way to finish a race is to...
A Keep running until you fall.
B Walk for a few minutes more. Then stretch well and relax.
C Go straight to bed.

Sweaty
... to nice and clean

If you've been running around, you're probably hot and sweaty. Make sure you drink plenty of water so you don't dehydrate.

Wash thoroughly to refresh yourself. Take a shower, dry well all over and change into some clean clothes. If you don't wash, you will cool down in your sweaty clothes. Germs love sweat. Wash and dry your feet properly. Otherwise, you might get an infection such as **athlete's foot**. And worst of all – you might become horribly smelly! Now sit down, relax and recover your strength.

Don't just use a deodorant. This will only hide the smell. Wash and dry well, especially your armpits, groin and feet.

3 Washing well after sports is very important because...
A You feel hot and sticky.
B Your teacher says you should.
C You can splash each other.

Remember, always drink plenty of water during exercise so you don't dehydrate.

ANSWERS: 1C, 2B, 3A.

Look forward to...
A healthy life

keep up your activities. Try out different ones, too. Get active for a month. Now go back to the beginning of the book. Try the fitness tests on pages 6 and 7 again. Can you see a difference? Are you any faster, stronger or fitter after doing regular exercise?

◄ *Don't let the rain put you off. Just get wellington boots and an umbrella and jump over the puddles.*

Fitness facts

Or try this...

When there's a crowd...
- Learn disco-dancing or tap-dancing.
- Join a football or netball team.
- Play water volleyball.

be active every day

Stay active...

Do you like running through the fields with your dog? Or climbing a mountain? Do you like digging sand castles or flying a kite? Whatever you do – remember it's important to 'get active'. Just 20 minutes a day makes all the difference. You'll be happy, and have lots of fun.

...all your life

Run and jump over hurdles, hedges, tree stumps, fences, low walls...

2 vary your activities

3 at least 20 minutes exercise a day

When there's just two of you...
● Go for a bike ride together.
● Go on a nature walk. Collect different types of leaves and flowers and look at the wildlife.

When you're on your own...
● Practise skipping with a rope.
● Go for a jog and time yourself on a stopwatch.
● Help your parents with the chores.

Glossary

What does it mean ?

activity: *An activity is anything you do when you are active. It could be a game you play, or a sport you practise, or helping your parents with the housework, for example.*

asthma: *A common chest disease that makes breathing difficult. It is often caused or made worse by allergies.*

athlete's foot: *A fungus that lives in the moist places between toes. The skin cracks and gets very itchy.*

diabetes: *A diabetic cannot control the levels of sugar in her or his blood and needs to take special medicine.*

heart: *An important organ inside your chest. It pumps blood around your body. Blood carries oxygen from the lungs to where it is needed in the body.*

joints: *The 'hinges' where two bones connect. We have joints in our shoulders, knees, wrists and ankles, for example.*

lungs: *Two organs inside our chests. We use our lungs to breathe in and out.*

organs: *Parts of our bodies. We have organs on the inside of our bodies (brain, heart, lungs, stomach, kidneys) and on the outside (ears, eyes, nose). Each organ has a certain job.*

oxygen: *An important part of the air that we breathe. We need oxygen to live.*

spine: *A line of connected bones down the centre of your back. It supports your body.*

To find out more...

...check out these websites

- www.bbc.co.uk/health
The BBC website containing articles and news about all aspects of health.

- www.kidshealth.org
A great website with lots of health info.
- www.childrenshealth.co.uk
- www.childrenshealth.org.uk

To find out more...

...read these books

● Ganeri, Anita. *How My Body Works: Moving.* The Evans Publishing Group, 2006.

● Gaff, Jackie. *Why Must I...Take Exercise?* Cherrytree Books, 2005

● *Look After Yourself* KS2 CD Rom. Evans Publishing Group, 2006.

● Royston, Angela. *Look After Yourself: Get Some Exercise.* Heinemann Library, 2003.

● Lobb, Janice. *Bump! Thump! How Do We Jump?* Kingfisher, 2000.

● Ballard, Carol. *Keeping Healthy: Exercise.* Hodder Wayland, 2004.

● Powell, Jillian. *Health Matters: Exercise and Your Health.* Hodder Wayland, 2002.

● Spilsbury, Louise. *Why Should I Get Off the Sofa? And Other Questions about Health and Exercise.* Heinemann Library, 2004.

● Guber, Tara. *Yoga Pretzels: 50 Fun Activities for Kids and Grown-Ups.* Barefoot Books, 2005.

www.kidzworld.com
www.wheelpower.org.uk
www.getkidsgoing.com/homepage.tml - Get Kids Going has information about children (and adults) with disabilities getting into all different types of sport.

Index

Which page is it on?